Edition Schott

Alvin Singleton
*1940

ARGORU I

for Piano
für Klavier

Edited by/Herausgegeben von
Laura Gordy

ED 30022
ISMN M-60001-055-4

www.schott-music.com

Mainz · London · Madrid · New York · Paris · Prague · Tokyo · Toronto
© 1970 SCHOTT MUSIC CORPORATION, New York · Printed in USA

Preface

The word *argoru* comes from the Ghanaian Twi language and means "to play." ARGORU I for piano is the first in a series of virtuoso pieces for solo instruments, including cello, flute, viola, bass clarinet, alto flute, marimba, vibraphone and snare drum. To play ARGORU I, the performer must be prepared to explore complex rhythmic and melodic gestures and sudden shifts of dynamics and range. The melodic lines bounce along like atonal jazz riffs, violently interrupted by clusters that serve as tonal pillars. The material is precisely notated until it climaxes in a burst of controlled improvisation. An intellectually rigorous work, ARGORU I nevertheless maintains a playfulness and spontaneity. ARGORU I was composed for pianist Lea Bissell and was premiered on May 1, 1970 in Sprague Memorial Hall at Yale University.

Laura Gordy
2009

Vorwort

Das Wort „argoru" kommt aus dem Dialekt Twi, welcher in Ghana gesprochen wird, und übersetzt schlicht „spielen" bedeutet. ARGORU I für Klavier ist der erste Teil einer Serie virtuoser Stücke für Soloinstrumente, wie Cello, Flöte, Viola, Bassklarinette, Altflöte, Marimba, Vibraphon und kleine Trommel. Um ARGORU I zu spielen, muss der Ausführende bereit sein, komplexe Rhythmen, sowie melodische Gesten und unerwartete Verschiebungen in der Dynamik und im Tonumfang zu erkunden. Die melodischen Linien springen vorüber, wie atonale Jazz-riffs, die von heftigen Clustern unterbrochen werden, welche als tonale Säulen dienen. Das Material ist präzise notiert, bis es schließlich im Höhepunkt kontrollierter Improvisation zerplatzt. Ein gedanklich rigoroses Werk, gleichwohl ARGORU I durchweg eine Verspieltheit und Ungezwungenheit enthält. ARGORU I wurde für die Pianistin Lea Bissell komponiert und am 1. Mai 1970 in der Sprague Memorial Hall der Yale Universität uraufgeführt.

Laura Gordy
2009
Translation by Thorsten Schlotterbeck

to Lea

ARGORU I

Alvin Singleton

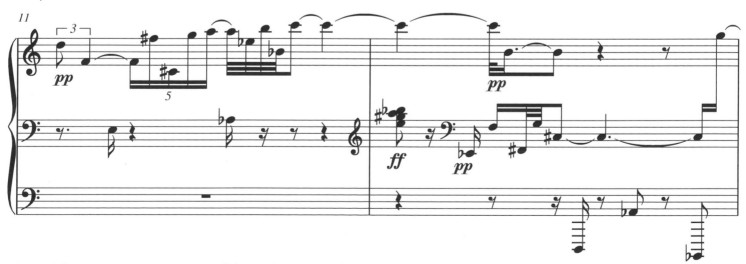

ED30022

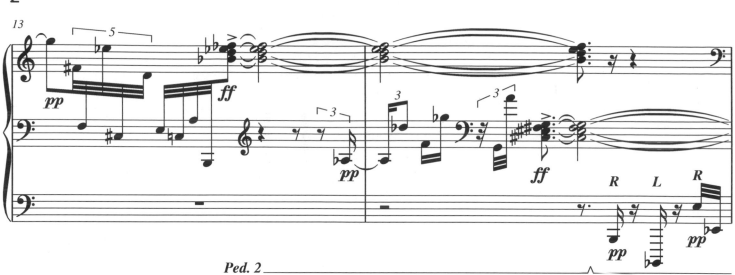

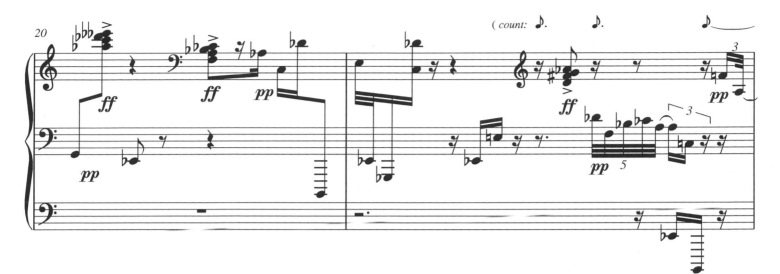

4

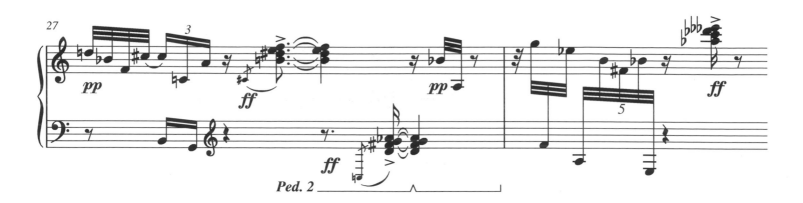

* To be played as a chromatic cluster, range indicated by rectangle.

Senza misura

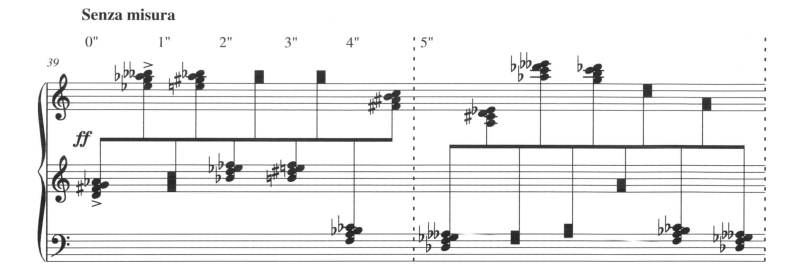

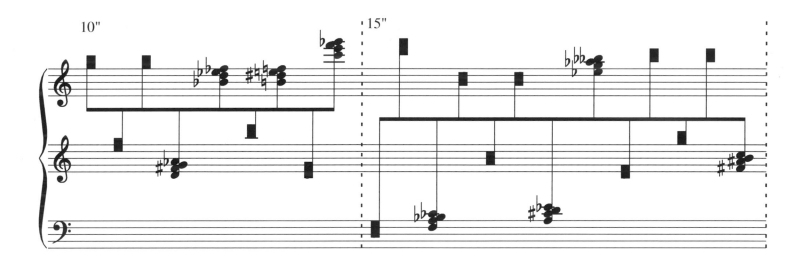

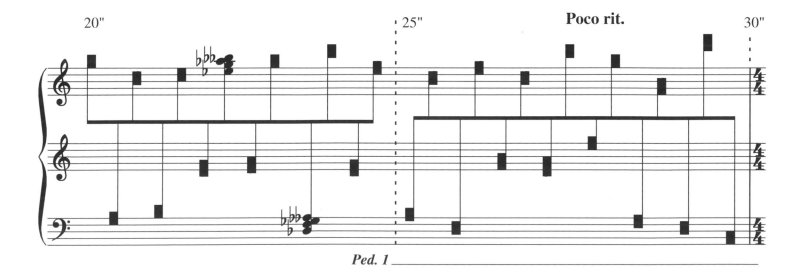

Ped. 1

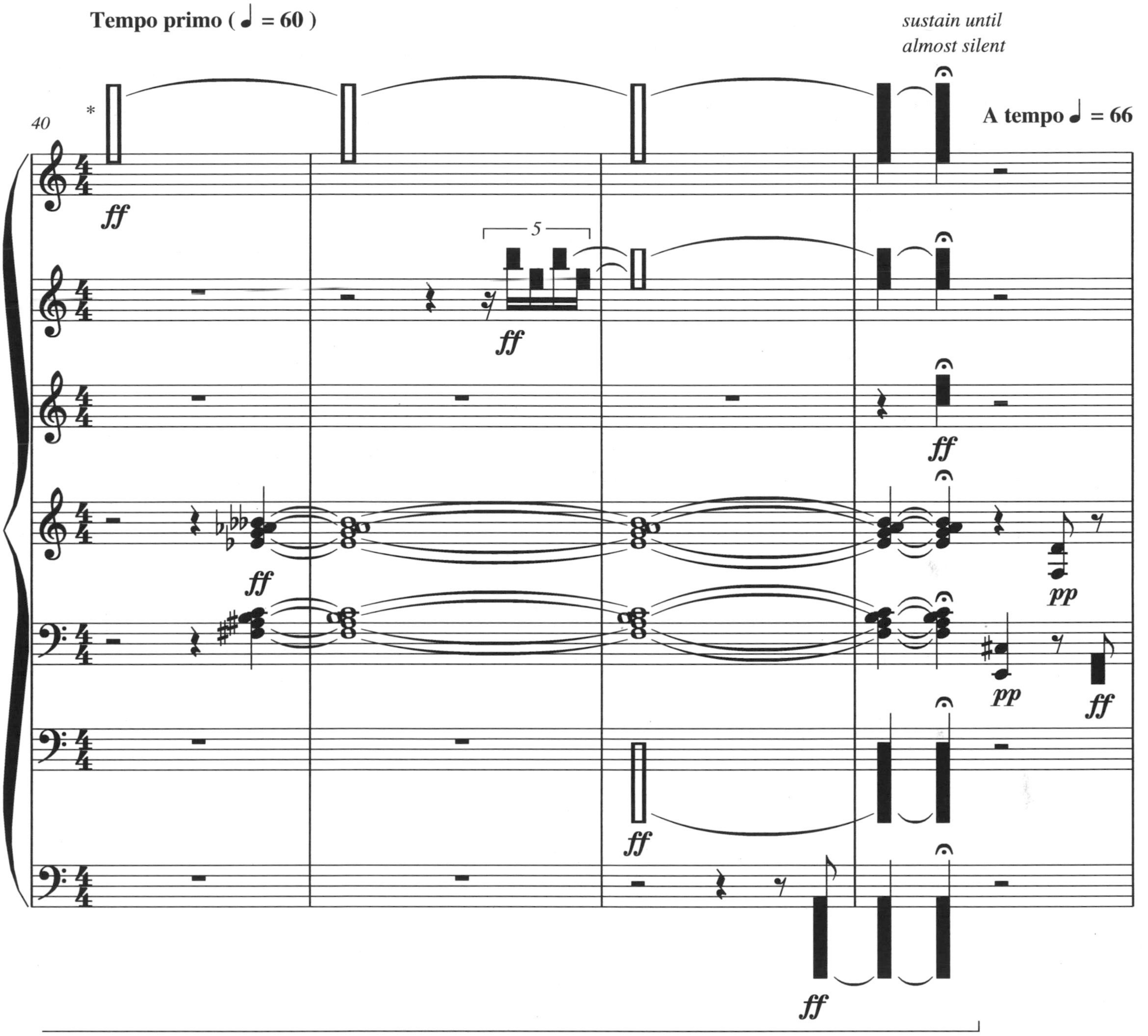

Tempo primo (♩ = 60)

sustain until
almost silent

40

A tempo ♩ **= 66**

ff

5

ff

ff

ff

ff

pp

pp

ff

ff

ff

* *to be played with forearms.*

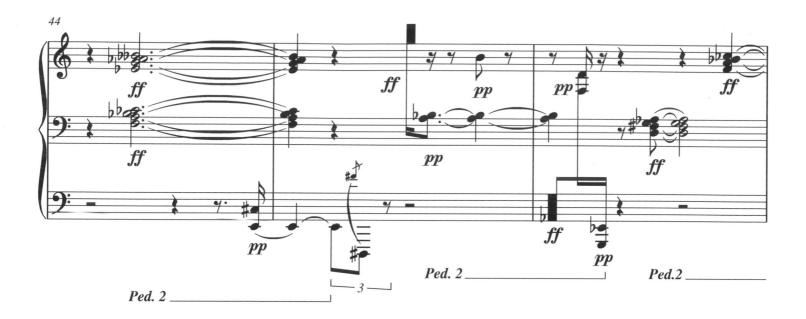

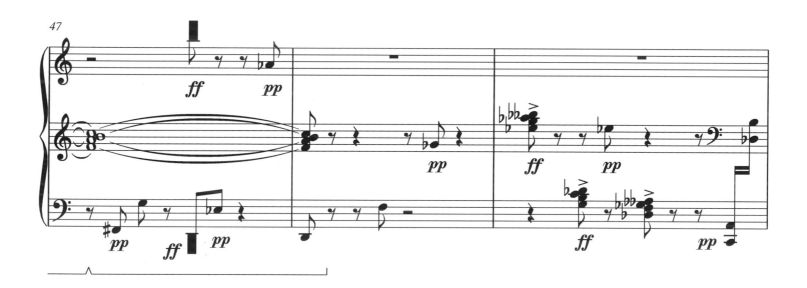

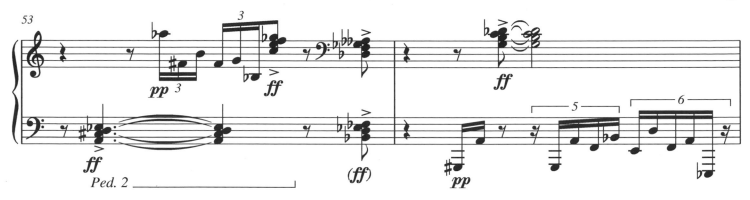

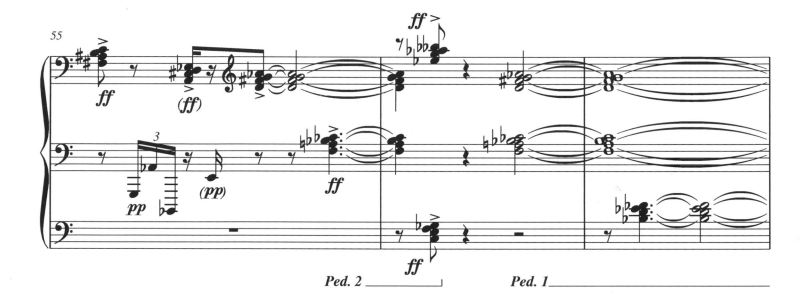

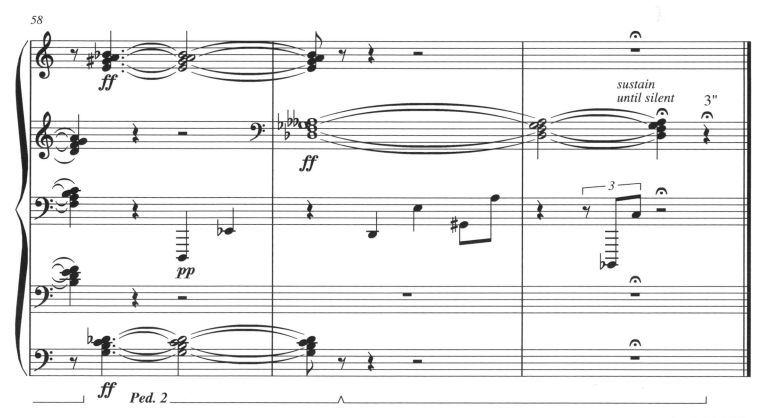

April 17, 1970
New Haven, Connecticut